You Can Stop Bullying

180 Dilemmas for Elementary Students

Darylann Whitemarsh, Ph.D.

Copyright © 2019 Darylann Whitemarsh, Ph.D.

All rights reserved. No part of this publication may be reproduced or transmitted in any form or by any electronic or mechanical means including photo copying, recording, or any information storage and retrieval system now known or to be invented, without permission in writing from the publisher or the author.

ISBN-13: 978-1-945976-25-4

Published by EA Books Publishing, a division of
Living Parables of Central Florida, Inc. a 501c3

EABooksPublishing.com

DEDICATION

I would like to dedicate this book to all the children who have been, and are being harassed and bullied in their schools and personal life. After reading this book, you will have a quiet confidence that it is not you, but others who have a problem. You now have the framework to understand the problem, and act in a positive way to any situation

TABLE OF CONTENTS

Dilemma 1: Cookie Thief 4

Dilemma 2: Teachers Desk 5

Dilemma 3: Carving on Desk 6

Dilemma 4: Scribbles on Paper 7

Dilemma 5: Recess Rules 8

Dilemma 6: Name on Paper 9

Dilemma 7: Weapon in School 10

Dilemma 8: Stealing 11

Dilemma 9: Honesty 12

Dilemma 10: Drugs 13

Dilemma 11: Gossip 14

Dilemma 12: Fire Alarm 15

Dilemma 13: Cheating 16

Dilemma 14: Recess Problem 17

Dilemma 15: Backpack Issue 18

Dilemma 16: Homework 19

Dilemma 17: Stealing 20

Dilemma 18: Lunch 21

Dilemma 19: Field Trip 22

Dilemma 20: Cupcakes 23

Dilemma 21: Playground Issues 24

Dilemma 22: Snack Time 25

Dilemma 23: Reading Time 26

Dilemma 24: Student Desk 27

Dilemma 25: Flying Peas 28

Dilemma 26: Taking without Asking 20

Dilemma 27: Student Tripping 30

Dilemma 28: Math Class 31

Dilemma 29: Tapping Fingers 32

Dilemma 30: Candy Sale 33

Dilemma 31: Bathroom 34

Dilemma 32: Best Friend Issue 35

Dilemma 33: Dirty Words 36

Dilemma 34: Lunch Room Issues 37

Dilemma 35: Stealing Food 38

Dilemma 36: Pushing and Shoving 39

Dilemma 37: New Student 40

Dilemma 38: Running Fingers 41

Dilemma 39: Skipping School 42

Dilemma 40: Paper Stealing 43

Dilemma 41: Bathroom Glue 44

Dilemma 42: Rumors 45

Dilemma 43: School Bus 46

Dilemma 44: Art Class 47

Dilemma 45: Poking Fun 48

Dilemma 46: Water Fountain 49

Dilemma 47: Arguing 50

Dilemma 48: Put Downs 51

Dilemma 49: Homework Binder 52

Dilemma 50: Tell the Truth 53

Dilemma 51: Overweight 54

Dilemma 52: Vandalism 55

Dilemma 53: Parent Issues 56

Dilemma 54: Student Diabetic 57

Dilemma 55: School Break 58

Dilemma 56: Birthday Parties 59

Dilemma 57:	Children of Faith	60
Dilemma 58:	Money Missing	61
Dilemma 59:	Learns Differently	62
Dilemma 60:	Stutters	63
Dilemma 61:	Picking on Students	64
Dilemma 62:	Student Issues	65
Dilemma 63:	Student Smirk	66
Dilemma 64:	Lunch Line	67
Dilemma 65:	Girl's Club	68
Dilemma 66:	Sarcastic Remark	69
Dilemma 67:	Don't Know Answer	70
Dilemma 68:	Pushing and Falling	71
Dilemma 69:	Recess Prank	72
Dilemma 70:	Student Inappropriate Behavior	73
Dilemma 71:	Poking Fun	74
Dilemma 72:	Spiked Hair	75
Dilemma 73:	Dirty Shoes	76
Dilemma 74:	Bathroom Paddle	77
Dilemma 75:	Looks Sad	78
Dilemma 76:	Put Downs	79
Dilemma 77:	Poking Fun	80
Dilemma 78:	Duck Decoys	81
Dilemma 79:	Library Book	82
Dilemma 80:	Interrupting	83
Dilemma 81:	Bathroom	84
Dilemma 82:	Gym Clothes	85
Dilemma 83:	Cheating	86
Dilemma 84:	Lunchtime	87
Dilemma 85:	Lying, Hitting and Pushing	88

Dilemma 86: Sitting Alone 89

Dilemma 87: Lying 90

Dilemma 88: Cheating 91

Dilemma 89: Fire Alarm 92

Dilemma 90: Spelling Test 93

Dilemma 91: Classroom Computer 94

Dilemma 92: Science Assignment 95

Dilemma 93: Missing Shoes 96

Dilemma 94: No Friends 97

Dilemma 95: Sleepover 98

Dilemma 96: Math Test 99

Dilemma 97: Missing Soda 100

Dilemma 98: Jacket on Chair 101

Dilemma 99: Lunchtime Mess 102

Dilemma 100: Bathroom Sink 103

Dilemma 101: Bow your Head 104

Dilemma 102: Your Friend 105

Dilemma 103: Case of Acne 106

Dilemma 104: School Violence 107

Dilemma 105: Bathroom Mark Up 108

Dilemma 106: Peer Problems 109

Dilemma 107: Cheating 110

Dilemma 108: Wednesday Night Commitment 111

Dilemma 109: Lying 112

Dilemma 110: Recess Time Games 113

Dilemma 111: Hitting People 114

Dilemma 112: Forgotten Pencil 115

Dilemma 113: Clean-Up Mess 116

Dilemma 114: Interrupts People 117

Dilemma 115: Promises 118

Dilemma 116: Game Time 119

Dilemma 117: Student Threat 120

Dilemma 118: Laughing at Peer 121

Dilemma 119: Teams 122

Dilemma 120: Class Bully 123

Dilemma 121: Student Punching 124

Dilemma 122: Stealing 125

Dilemma 123: Lunch time 126

Dilemma 124: Bathroom Vandalism 127

Dilemma 125: Friend who Bullies 128

Dilemma 126: Spit Balls 129

Dilemma 127: Bathroom 130

Dilemma 128: Teacher Desk 131

Dilemma 129: Toilet Paper 132

Dilemma 130: Gossip 133

Dilemma 131: Holiday Break Mishap 134

Dilemma 132: Snack Time Bully 135

Dilemma 133: Bathroom Stalls 136

Dilemma 134: Spelling Test 137

Dilemma 135: Screaming Boys 138

Dilemma 136: Holiday Concert 139

Dilemma 137: Running in Hall 140

Dilemma 138: Gun Bag 141

Dilemma 139: School Bully 142

Dilemma 140: Mean Comments 143

Dilemma 141: Stealing 144

Dilemma 142: Acted Out 145

Dilemma 143: Pokes Students 146

Dilemma 144 : Front of Lunch Line 147

Dilemma 145: Bad Words 148

Dilemma 146: Cigarettes 149

Dilemma 147: Lying 150

Dilemma 148: Team Assignment 151

Dilemma 149: Teacher Desk 152

Dilemma 150: Math Games 153

Dilemma 151: Homework 154

Dilemma 152: Learns Differently 155

Dilemma 153: Recess Smoking 156

Dilemma 154: Special Pen Case 157

Dilemma 155: Substitute Teacher 158

Dilemma 156: Gum Chewing 159

Dilemma 157: Struggling Friend 160

Dilemma 158: Spreading Lies 161

Dilemma 159: Wrong Procedure 162

Dilemma 160: Borrows Pencils 163

Dilemma 161: Missing Candy 164

Dilemma 162: Reading Struggle 165

Dilemma 163: Short Skirt Test 166

Dilemma 164: Gossiping 167

Dilemma 165: Gun in School 168

Dilemma 166: School Bus 169

Dilemma 167: Rainbow Hair 170

Dilemma 168: Gym Class 171

Dilemma 169: Lunch Time 172

Dilemma 170: Stealing 173

Dilemma 171: Learns Differently 174

Dilemma 172: Lunchtime 175

Dilemma 173:	Pokes and Pushes	176
Dilemma 174:	New Library Books	177
Dilemma 175:	School Violence	178
Dilemma 176:	Mean Comments	179
Dilemma 177:	Speech Problem	180
Dilemma 178:	Not Prepared	181
Dilemma 179:	Cheating	182
Dilemma 180:	Assignment Problem	183

PREFACE

You Can Stop Bullying is centered around age- appropriate, real-life dilemmas that a student can discuss with a parent, teacher or friend and write-out and explain their decision. This is a practical, what-if book that draws the student to question what bullying is and how he or she can be the solution to the problem in a positive way. After reading and applying the book, the student has a strong grasp on what it means to be a respectful and responsible person every day.

This book can be used by teachers and parents to guide students in making right choices. These are real-life bullying dilemmas that students face every day in their personal or school life. Having a teacher guide student in discussions, writing activities or integrate into the curriculum will help students understand what bullying is and how to respond.

Parents are partners in providing guidance to their child and can work hand-in-hand with the teacher in teaching their child how to respond to bullying dilemmas. Working together, both teacher and parent will help children to overcome bullying..

INTRODUCTION

Have you ever seen or heard unkind and mean behaviors in your school? Maybe you have seen students being unfriendly, disrespectful to other students, teachers, or their parents. What about someone hitting, punching, or kicking another student? Another area that shows up in school that you may have seen or heard is someone spreading rumors or calling someone a bad name. When you see or hear this, how does it make you feel? You may not be the victim now, but you witness this and wonder, when am I the next one to be picked on?

Bullying happens in all schools. What you just read are ways bullying occurs. You know bullying is happening, but you ask yourself, "What can I do about it?" In this book there are examples of bullying dilemmas that you face during your 180 days in school. Bullying dilemmas of all kinds are used by a bully to hurt other people or to make themselves feel better about themselves.

What is a dilemma? A dilemma is a real-life situation that happens where you have to make a very difficult choice between two or more options. You could also think of a dilemma as a tough, hard-to-solve situation or problem. The dilemmas you read and answer in this book are real and have happened in elementary schools just like yours. Here you get to write your own answer to how you would solve the dilemma on each page. That way you will learn about real-life situations where bullying occurs, understand it better, become a person who can make the right choices, and learn how to respond to a bully or a bullying situation.

After you have read the dilemma and thinking about how to solve the dilemma, how do you know you are making the right decision? What did you use to guide your decision? Here are some ways that will help guide you in your decision-making process:

- Talk with your parents about the dilemma and get their opinion.

- Talk with your teacher and ask him or her if your choice makes sense and if it's leading you to be a person of character. (A person of character is respectful and responsible.)

- If you have brothers or sisters, read the dilemmas with them, and all of you can decide on a good response.

- Discuss with your parents or teacher what a person of character is or is not?

- Ask your teacher if you can use these dilemmas to discuss with the entire class.

- If you are faith based, use this as your foundation for solving your dilemmas

- Ask yourself: What does a good person do in this situation? What is the right thing to do?

All of these will help lead you to a clear response to your dilemma. Remember that you can use more than one of these processes to decide if you made the right choice. That means you can talk with your parents or teacher to help you solve these dilemmas.

When you start reading the dilemmas, you need a plan to understand what you can do to solve them. Try these four steps: **Think, Decide, Act, Reflect (T-D-A-R)**

Think: After you have read the dilemma, think about it and decide if it's right or wrong for a person to do this.

Decide: Next, decide exactly what you would do. In other words, "what steps will you take to make the right choice in solving this dilemma?"

Act: Then, once you have made your decision of what to do, act on your decision. Do what you think is best.

Reflect: After you have solved the dilemma, ask yourself "Did my response move me in the right direction?"

Remember as you read the dilemmas, you are trying to understand and see what bullying is so you can react and respond to any dilemma in a positive way now and in the future

180 DILEMMAS FOR ELEMENTARY STUDENTS

Dilemma 1: Cookie Thief

Susan goes to her backpack at snack time and finds her cookie missing. This makes her really mad, because she is hungry. She sees Mike eating a cookie just like hers. She doesn't know if the cookie he is eating is hers or if Mike would go in her backpack and take her cookie. What would you do?

Write what you would do or how you would help. Explain why.

Dilemma 2: Teachers Desk

Two students are standing at the teacher's desk. One student quickly slips several of the teacher's pencils and pens into his pocket without anyone noticing. You see it and know it's wrong. What do you do?

Write what you would do or how you would help. Explain why.

Dilemma 3: Carving on Desk

In class you see a student carving a name on the corner of a desk. What would you do?

Write what you would do or how you would help. Explain why.

Dilemma 4: Scribbles on Paper

Jason walks by your desk and leans down, and scribbles on your paper. What would you do?

Write what you would do or how you would help. Explain why.

Dilemma 5: Recess Rules

Recess is over and everyone is bringing in their supplies except one student. He was on first base and the ball and bat are still there. He knows he was supposed to bring in the ball and bat after recess. What would you do?

Write what you would do or how you would help. Explain why.

Dilemma 6: Name on Paper

You are in a hurry to hand in your homework and forget to put your name on it. The teacher asks you where your homework is and you tell her that you handed it in. She brings the papers over so you can look through them and you see that the student behind you put his name on your paper. What do you do?

Write what you would do or how you would help. Explain why.

Dilemma 7: Weapon in School

You are sitting in your desk watching the teacher and a student in front of you opens his desk and you see a weapon. What do you do?

Write what you would do or how you would help. Explain why.

Dilemma 8: Stealing

It's recess time and three people are in the classroom, you and two other students. You see two students taking things off the teacher's desk and putting them in their backpack. What would you do?

Write what you would do or how you would help. Explain why.

Dilemma 9: Honesty

Your best friend asks you to be on her team, but you already are on a team. You don't want to hurt her feelings by telling her no. What do you do?

Write what you would do or how you would help. Explain why.

Dilemma 10: Drugs

It's Friday afternoon and you can't wait to get home and play. At recess you overhear some students say they are going to smoke some pot in the far corner of the playground. What would you do?

Write what you would do or how you would help. Explain why.

Dilemma 11: Gossip

You have many friends in your class. You love being around all of them. One of the friends starts talking bad about other class members and wants you to be friends only with him. What would you do?

Write what you would do or how you would help. Explain why.

Dilemma 12: Fire alarm

You find a handwritten note on the floor and pick it up. You open the note and read that the school fire alarm will be pulled at 11:00 am. What would you do?

Write what you would do or how you would help. Explain why.

Dilemma 13: Cheating

Your social studies test is in an hour and you didn't study for the test. You sit next to a smart classmate and know you can cheat off his paper. Do you try and cheat or ask the teacher for an extra day to study? What would you do?

Write what you would do or how you would help. Explain why.

Dilemma 14: Recess Problem

During recess you see another student hitting and pushing a student? What would you do?

Write what you would do or how you would help. Explain why.

Dilemma 15: Backpack issue

You turn around in your seat and see another student reaching into another student's backpack and taking out a candy bar. What would you do?

Write what you would do or how you would help. Explain why.

Dilemma 16: Homework

It's Monday morning and you didn't complete any homework over the weekend. You see that the student next to you has done the work and you could easily copy the papers. What would you do?

Write what you would do or how you would help. Explain why.

Dilemma 17: Stealing

Sharon is putting on her coat to leave for the day. Then she walks over to another student's locker, opens it, and takes the gloves sitting on the top shelf. You see all of this. What would you do?

Write what you would do or how you would help. Explain why.

Dilemma 18: Lunch

Mike walks into the lunch room with his class. They all take seats at tables together, except for one student who appears to be unwanted. He is left to sit by himself at another table. What could you do?

Write what you would do or how you would help. Explain why.

Dilemma 19: Field Trip

Students are on a field trip. On the bus students are singing and laughing loudly. Then you see a student repeatedly poking a student who learns differently. What would you do?

Write what you would do or how you would help. Explain why.

Dilemma 20: Cupcakes

A student's mom brought cupcakes to your class for a treat. Each student in the class is given one cupcake. You are sitting in the back of the class doing an assignment. You see a student take a cupcake off the desk of a student who is sitting in the back of the class. What would you do?

Write what you would do or how you would help. Explain why.

Dilemma 21: Playground Issues

Three students are playing a game on the playground. A fourth student wants to join them. You know this student has difficulty with making friends. What do you do?

Write what you would do or how you would help. Explain why.

Dilemma 22: Snack Time

It's snack time and one student brought candy to share with some students, but not all students. There are students in the class who don't have any snacks and are just sitting there looking sad. What would you do?

Write what you would do or how you would help. Explain why.

Dilemma 23: Reading Time

Reading time begins everyday at 11:00 am for fifteen minutes. Students can sit anywhere in the room on the floor, bean bags or their desks. What would you do if you saw a students laughing at the book choice a student made?

Write what you would do or how you would help. Explain why.

Dilemma 24: Student Desk

Students have a habit of taking items out of other students' desks without asking them. How would you feel if someone took something out of your desk that you thought was special? What would you do?

Write what you would do or how you would help. Explain why.

Dilemma 25: Flying Peas

At lunch you see a student put his peas on a spoon and send the peas flying hitting another student on the head. The student who was hit with the peas got up and ran over to hit the boy. What would you do?

Write what you would do or how you would help. Explain why.

Dilemma 26: Taking Without Asking

You have an assignment due the next day, but you know you don't have any paper, glue, or markers to complete the assignment. You go into the storage closet and take what you need without asking. Your friend sees you do this. What would you do?

Write what you would do or how you would help. Explain why.

Dilemma 27: Student Tripping

Students are coming into the class. You see a student sitting at his desk and sticking out his leg tripping students. What would you do?

Write what you would do or how you would help. Explain why.

Dilemma 28: Math Class

A student in math class has been taking things out of student's desks. You discover who is doing this. What would you do?

Write what you would do or how you would help. Explain why.

Dilemma 29: Tapping Fingers

A student has a habit of tapping his fingers on the desk during class. It's annoying to you. What would you do?

Write what you would do or how you would help. Explain why.

Dilemma 30: Candy Sale

Wednesday is candy sale day. Rachel doesn't have any money to buy candy but takes some candy anyway. George sees her take the candy. What would you do?

Write what you would do or how you would help. Explain why.

Dilemma 31: Bathroom

During reading class, a student asks to use the bathroom. He seems to go to the bathroom every Wednesday at 11:00 am. You know he is meeting his friends in the bathroom to goof off. What would you do?

Write what you would do or how you would help. Explain why.

Dilemma 32: Best Friend Issue

You heard from a friend that your best friend is telling students that you took a cookie off the treat table without asking. You know this isn't true. What would you do?

Write what you would do or how you would help. Explain why.

Dilemma 33: Dirty Words

A boy in class whispers in your ear some dirty words. You tell him to stop but he doesn't listen to you. He keeps this up every day. What would you do?

Write what you would do or how you would help. Explain why.

Dilemma 34: Lunch Room Issues

Students are lined up for lunch. Jane barges in and goes to the front of the line without the teacher noticing. What could you do?

Write what you would do or how you would help. Explain why.

Dilemma 35: Stealing Food

Your teacher has a small refrigerator in the classroom. You see a student going in and stealing her food. What would you do?

Write what you would do or how you would help. Explain why.

Dilemma 36: Pushing and Shoving

You are walking back from lunch and see two students pushing each other. The teacher comes by and stops them. She asks the students who started this. You saw the pushing. What would you do?

Write what you would do or how you would help. Explain why.

Dilemma 37: New Student

A new student just came to the school. She seems really nice and you want to be friends with her. One of your friends tells you she heard that the girl is from the wrong side of the tracks and not to be friends with her. What would you do?

Write what you would do or how you would help. Explain why.

Dilemma 38: Running Fingers

A boy takes his fingers and runs them up and down the back of a girl that sits in from of him in class. The girl tells him to stop but he doesn't. What should the girl do?

Write what you would do or how you would help. Explain why.

Dilemma 39: Skipping School

A student is bragging that he's not coming to school next week because he's going hunting with his brother. There is a no skipping school policy at your school. What would you do?

Write what you would do or how you would help. Explain why.

Dilemma 40: Paper Stealing

A boy in your class is using his brother's papers from last year's class. He is making straight A's and you are struggling. He asks you if you want to use his brother's papers. What would you do?

Write what you would do or how you would help. Explain why.

Dilemma 41: Bathroom Glue

A student is seen putting glue on the toilet seats in the girl's bathroom. You know who is doing this. What would you do?

Write what you would do or how you would help. Explain why.

Dilemma 42: Rumors

Two girls in your gym class are spreading untrue rumors about a girl and you know that the rumors are untrue. What would you do?

Write what you would do or how you would help. Explain why.

Dilemma 43: School Bus

Two boys on the school bus hit you with their fists as you get on board. This happens almost every day. You don't want to nark on them but it hurts to get hit on the arm. What would you do?

Write what you would do or how you would help. Explain why.

Dilemma 44: Art Class

You see two students take the spray paint out of the art classroom and go outside and spray paint on the outside of the building. The teacher asks who did it. What would you do?

Write what you would do or how you would help. Explain why.

Dilemma 45: Poking Fun

A group of students are poking fun of you because you went to church on Sunday. These same students pick on students who go to church on Saturday. What would you do?

Write what you would do or how you would help. Explain why.

Dilemma 46: Water Fountain

You are standing in line at the water fountain and a boy turns and spits water on you. What would you do?

Write what you would do or how you would help. Explain why.

Dilemma 47: Arguing

You hear two students arguing over a pencil case. Each student says it is theirs. The teacher overhears the arguing and asks what is going on. You know who owns the pencil case. What do you do?

Write what you would do or how you would help. Explain why.

Dilemma 48: Put Downs

A boy in your class likes to make fun of people by putting them down and having other people laugh with him at the poor victim's fate. You know this is wrong. What would you do?

Write what you would do or how you would help. Explain why.

Dilemma 49: Homework Binder

You forgot to have your parents sign your homework binder. So you decide to sign it yourself. The teacher questions you about the signature. Should you tell the truth and why you did it? What would you do?

Write what you would do or how you would help. Explain why.

Dilemma 50: To Tell the Truth

You forgot your homework, and the teacher wants to know why. Do you lie or tell her the truth? What would you do?

Write what you would do or how you would help. Explain why.

Dilemma 51: Overweight

A student who is overweight is being picked on in class. You see this and are disgusted. The student doesn't want to come to school anymore. What would you do?

Write what you would do or how you would help. Explain why.

Dilemma 52: Vandalism

A student takes lipstick and scribbles swear words on the bathroom mirrors. You and two other students are in the bathroom when this happened. What would you do?

Write what you would do or how you would help. Explain why.

Dilemma 53: Parent Issues

A student in your class tells you he hates his mom and dad and wants them dead. He tells you they should burn. What would you do?

Write what you would do or how you would help. Explain why.

Dilemma 54: Student Diabetic

You see a student in class acting strange. You know he is a diabetic and has diabetic lows from time to time. He starts shaking and jerking. What would you do?

Write what you would do or how you would help. Explain why.

Dilemma 55: School Break

It's the holiday season and you'll soon go home for a school break. You want to hand-out presents to some students but not all of them. What do you do?

Write what you would do or how you would help. Explain why.

Dilemma 56: Birthday Parties

When the school year is starting you know what is coming, student birthday parties. What would you do if someone in your class didn't get an invitation to a party, but everyone else in the class did? You saw this happen last school year and how it hurt some students who didn't get an invitation. What would you do?

Write what you would do or how you would help. Explain why.

Dilemma 57: Children of Faith

A friend of yours goes to Wednesday night Bible study and another friend attends a mosque for worship. Some kids in class find out and start making fun of them for this. What would you do?

Write what you would do or how you would help. Explain why.

Dilemma 58: Money Missing

A teacher opens her desk drawer and discovers her lunch money is missing. You saw who took the money. What would you do?

Write what you would do or how you would help. Explain why.

Dilemma 59: Learns Differently

A student who learns differently is struggling to understand the assignment. Some students in class don't want to work with him because they know they would have to explain the directions to him. You see the student get red in the face from embarrassment. What would you do?

Write what you would do or how you would help. Explain why.

Dilemma 60: Stutters

Every time Mack is called on in class, he stutters. Most students understand his situation, but a few giggles and mimic him. Mack says he doesn't want to go to school anymore. What could you do?

Write what you would do or how you would help. Explain why.

Dilemma 61: Picking on Students

A student in your class likes to poke people with his pencil. He thinks it's funny, but you don't. What can you do to help stop this?

Write what you would do or how you would help. Explain why.

Dilemma 62: Student Issues

During art class, three students are pushing the art supplies off the counter. These are the same art supplies everyone needs to use. The teacher asks who did this. You saw it but don't want to get involved. What do you do

Write what you would do or how you would help. Explain why.

Dilemma 63: Student Smirks

You ask another student in your class to explain the directions for the assignment to you. The student looks at you with a smirk on her face and says you should know how to figure this out. What would you do?

Write what you would do or how you would help. Explain why.

Dilemma 64: Lunch Line

Every day in the lunch line various kids push aside one particular student so they can go ahead of him. You always see this and it disgusts you. What would you do?

Write what you would do or how you would help. Explain why.

Dilemma 65: Girl's Club

You want to join a girls' club at school. You ask the club leader how to join and she says, "We don't want people like you in the club." You feel awful and walk away. What would you do?

Write what you would do or how you would help. Explain why.

Dilemma 66: Sarcastic Remark

In front of the whole class, the teacher makes fun of you for not knowing the answer to a math problem. What would you do?

Write what you would do or how you would help. Explain why.

Dilemma 67: Don't Know the Answer

During class the teacher asks you a math question, and you say you don't know. Then you hear a student say that you are dumb and that's why you don't know the answer. What would you do?

Write what you would do or how you would help. Explain why.

Dilemma 68: Pushing and Falling

You are waiting outside for the teacher to let you in the building for the day. When you hear the teacher call you into the building, you start moving forward and a student behind you pushes you and you trip and fall. What would you do?

Write what you would do or how you would help. Explain why.

Dilemma 69: Recess Prank

A student in your class can act weird at times. A group of boys want to play a prank on him during recess. You overhead what they are going to do. What would you do

Write what you would do or how you would help. Explain why.

Dilemma 70: Student Inappropriate Behavior

A student in class is too friendly to everyone. She is seen hugging and kissing students during class and on the playground. Students are uncomfortable but don't know what to do. What would you do?

Write what you would do or how you would help. Explain why.

Dilemma 71: Poking Fun

It's game day for a major league sports event and your favorite team is playing. Another student is wearing the opposing team's shirt and hat. You start making fun of his team. You call the student names and poke fun of his choice. Is this right? What would you do?

Write what you would do or how you would help. Explain why.

Dilemma 72: Spiked hair

A student has his hair spiked. He comes into class, and students start making fun of him by touching his hair and calling him names. What would you do?

Write what you would do or how you would help. Explain why.

Dilemma 73: Dirty Shoes

A student walks into class with the same dirty shoes she wears every day. You see a group of girls making fun of her shoes. What would you do?

Write what you would do or how you would help. Explain why.

Dilemma 74: Bathroom Paddle

A boy asks the teacher to use the bathroom. He takes the bathroom paddle and walks through the library hitting books with the paddle. The books land on the floor in disarray. When he comes back to class, he tells you what he did. What would you do?

Write what you would do or how you would help. Explain why.

Dilemma 75: Looks Sad

Steve comes into class looking really sad. The boy sitting next to him pats him on the back and laughingly says everything is going to be okay. He continues to make fun of him because of his sadness. What he doesn't know is that Steve's dad died last Monday. What would you do?

Write what you would do or how you would help. Explain why.

Dilemma 76: Put Downs

You have a friend who always puts you down. You hear him putting other kids down to. You like the person but are hurt by the put downs. What would you do?

Write what you would do or how you would help. Explain why.

Dilemma 77: Poking Fun

Lilly sucks her thumb throughout class time. The students see this and poke fun at her during recess and lunch time. What would you do to help Lilly? What would you do?

Write what you would do or how you would help. Explain why.

Dilemma 78: Duck Decoys

Matt brings his grandfather's duck decoys to school to show his fourth-grade class. When Matt walks out of the room you see a student take one and put it in his backpack. You know who did it. What would you do?

Write what you would do or how you would help. Explain why.

Dilemma 79: Library

You are in the library and see someone marking up a new library book. What would you do?

Write what you would do or how you would help. Explain why.

Dilemma 80: Interrupting

Sue is always talking in class and interrupting everyone when they speak. It really bugs me because I can't concentrate on what the teacher is saying. What should I do?

Write what you would do or how you would help. Explain why.

Dilemma 81: Bathroom

A student asks his teacher to go to the bathroom. You see him going in the opposite direction of the bathroom. What would you do?

Write what you would do or how you would help. Explain why.

Dilemma 82: Gym Clothes

You notice that a group of boys make fun of Mike's old gym clothes. Mike reacts by almost crying because of the harassment. What would you do?

Write what you would do or how you would help. Explain why.

Dilemma 83: Cheating

You see two students comparing their answers on a math assignment. One student is erasing his answers and copying the other student. What would you do?

Write what you would do or how you would help. Explain why.

Dilemma 84: Lunchtime

It's lunchtime and a student at the table has no lunch to eat. What could you do to help him? What would you do?

Write what you would do or how you would help. Explain why.

Dilemma 85: Lying, Hitting and Pushing

Four students accuse each other of hitting and pushing each other. You didn't see them do this, but they want you to lie about who did the hitting and pushing. What do you do?

Write what you would do or how you would help. Explain why.

Dilemma 86: Sitting Alone

A student is always seen sitting alone in the back of the lunchroom. He has the same old lunch bag with only an apple in it. He hangs his head looking embarrassed. What could you do to help him? What would you do?

Write what you would do or how you would help. Explain why.

Dilemma 87: Lying

A student is seen talking to the teacher about another student. You are close enough to hear and know he is lying about that student. What would you do?

Write what you would do or how you would help. Explain why.

Dilemma 88: Cheating

Your best friend is cheating on a test. You studied all weekend for the test so her cheating makes you feel really bad. What could you do?

Write what you would do or how you would help. Explain why.

Dilemma 89: Fire Alarm

A student pulled the fire alarm and ran, laughing. You saw this happen. What would you do?

Write what you would do or how you would help. Explain why.

Dilemma 90: Spelling Test

During a spelling test, you see a student reach in his desk to get a new pencil, but he really goes in to see the spelling words in his open notebook. What do you do?

Write what you would do or how you would help. Explain why.

Dilemma 91: Classroom Computer

When Tim uses the classroom computer, he goes on sites that are not allowed. When the teacher checks the computer and asks who did this, no one confesses, but you know who did it. What would you do?

Write what you would do or how you would help. Explain why.

Dilemma 92: Science Assignment

The science teacher read out the answers to the science assignment and students who were grading another students paper entered the grade on the paper and returned the paper to the student. Before assignments were turned in, two students were seen changing their science grade. Both students are in sports and know if they have a low grade they can't play in the next game. You have worked hard to keep your grades up so you can play sports. What would you do?

Write what you would do or how you would help. Explain why.

Dilemma 93: Missing Shoes

Marsha brings her new shoes to gym class. During the class she takes the shoes off because they were giving her blisters. She puts them in her gym locker but forgets to lock it. Another student comes in and sees this, and after Marsha leaves the locker room, that student steals the shoes. What would you do?

Write what you would do or how you would help. Explain why.

Dilemma 94: No Friends

A student always sits alone at lunchtime. You have tried to sit and eat with him, but he doesn't want to have a friend. Is there anything you could do to help this student? What would you do?

Write what you would do or how you would help. Explain why.

Dilemma 95: Sleepover

Tom is having a sleepover on Friday night. He invited everyone in the class but one person, John. You like both John and Tom and want to be friends with each of them. How would you handle this? What would you do?

Write what you would do or how you would help. Explain why.

Dilemma 96: Math Test

It's Sunday night and have a math test Monday morning. You didn't study and cannot afford to fail the test. Monday morning you tell your Mom you are sick and need to stay home. What could you have done instead of lying? What would you do?

Write what you would do or how you would help. Explain why.

Dilemma 97: Missing Soda

You have a bottle of soda in your backpack labeled with orange tape around it so you know it's yours. During lunch break you go to get the soda and it's gone. You see a student from your class drinking the same soda with the orange tape around it. What would you do?

Write what you would do or how you would help. Explain why.

Dilemma 98: Jacket on Chair

Mack goes into the classroom and notices that Sam left his jacket on the chair. Mack really likes that jacket, so he quickly takes it and runs out of the classroom and off school grounds. You see all of this. Sam comes running into the room to retrieve his coat and finds it was gone. What would you do?

Write what you would do or how you would help. Explain why.

Dilemma 99: Lunchtime Mess

It's lunchtime and Mack and Andy are at it again. Mack takes his apple and throws it at Stan. Stan lets out a yell and throws his sandwich at Andy. You are sitting at the table with these two boys. What would you do?

Write what you would do or how you would help. Explain why.

Dilemma 100: Bathroom Sink

John and Tim are jumping on the bathroom sinks and suddenly one sink breaks. They race past you out of the bathroom. You stand there speechless not knowing what to do. You want to be friends with these boys and be in the popular group. You know you should tell the teacher but don't want to lose them as friends. What would you do?

Write what you would do or how you would help. Explain why.

Dilemma 101: Bow your head

Praying before a meal is important to you and the right thing to do. At lunch you bow your head to pray and a group of students bully you that you are a religious nut. What would you do?

Write what you would do or how you would help. Explain why.

Dilemma 102: Your Friend

A good friend asks to see your answers to the math assignment. You say sure, not knowing that she is going to copy all of them. But you hesitate, you don't want to stop her because you want her as a friend. What would you do?

Write what you would do or how you would help. Explain why.

Dilemma 103: Case of Acne

Jean has a terrible case of acne, and today it turned red and scabby. She is totally embarrassed about this. You hear a boy start making fun of her face. Jean runs in the bathroom crying. What would you do?

Write what you would do or how you would help. Explain why.

Dilemma 104: School Violence

You hear a student say "I just want to die, and I'm going to take everyone is this awful school with me." What would you do?

Write what you would do or how you would help. Explain why.

Dilemma 105: Bathroom Mark Up

After recess, students use the bathroom before going back to class. A student takes his marker and marks up the bathroom stalls with swear words. You see him do this. What would you do?

Write what you would do or how you would help. Explain why.

Dilemma 106: Peer Problems

Mark is having problems with his best friend. This is far from the first time Mark has had problems with his peers/classmates. Is there anything you can do to help Mark? What would you do?

Write what you would do or how you would help. Explain why.

Dilemma 107: Cheating

You see Jason walk out of his science class and meet his best friend by the locker. Jason starts telling his best friend the answers to the science test that he had written on his arm. You see his best friend writing the answers on his arm. What would you do?

Write what you would do or how you would help. Explain why.

Dilemma 108: Wednesday Night Commitment

Your soccer coach calls a practice meeting for 6:00 PM on Wednesday night. Wednesday night is Bible study at your church. Do you skip your scheduled Bible study or go to soccer practice? What would you do?

Write what you would do or how you would help. Explain why.

Dilemma 109: Lying

You see Sue take a watch off of the teacher's desk. She takes the watch and puts the watch in Jane's desk so it looks as if Jane stole the watch. The teacher comes back and asks the class where her watch is, and Sue points to Jane. What would you do?

Write what you would do or how you would help. Explain why.

Dilemma 110: Recess Time Games

It's recess time, and your class is dividing into teams to play some games. Kathy says she doesn't want to play with anyone and goes in the corner of the playground. After recess you can hear Kathy complaining to the teacher that no one would play with her. What would you do?

Write what you would do or how you would help. Explain why.

Dilemma 111: Hitting People

Carla has a habit of hitting people in the arm. She thinks it's funny, but she hits hard. What would you do?

Write what you would do or how you would help. Explain why.

Dilemma 112: Forgotten Pencil

Joey forgets his pencil every day and repeatedly asks you if he can borrow one of your pencils. This is starting to annoy you. What would you do?

Write what you would do or how you would help. Explain why.

Dilemma 113: Clean-Up Mess

After art class, everyone puts their materials away and goes back to their seats. John always leaves a mess at his art table. He goes back to his seat and lets his team clean- up his mess. What would you do?

Write what you would do or how you would help. Explain why.

Dilemma 114: Interrupts People

Hazel always interrupts people in class when they are talking. Today in class she talked over students to get her point across. You know Hazel has good ideas, but so do others in class. What would you do?

Write what you would do or how you would help. Explain why.

Dilemma 115: Promises

Luke made a promise to you that he would walk home with you and then play a game. After school Luke said he changed his mind wanted to go swimming with friends. As a friend you feel betrayed. What would you do?

Write what you would do or how you would help. Explain why.

Dilemma 116: Game Time

During game time at school, you and two other friends are busy with your game. A fourth student comes up to your group and asks if he can join you. What would you do?

Write what you would do or how you would help. Explain why.

Dilemma 117: Student Threat

On the way to lunch you hear a student make a threat to another student. He said, "If you don't do what I say, I'll beat you up after school." What would you do?

Write what you would do or how you would help. Explain why.

Dilemma 118: Laughing at Peer

Your group of friends start laughing at a boy who limps. You know this is wrong, but hesitate to say anything. What would you do?

Write what you would do or how you would help. Explain why.

Dilemma 119: Teams

You finished science and now are going into social studies and the teacher tells you to move into teams. Your team gathers at the table and one student who learns differently joins your group. You know he has a difficult time reading, but you ask him to read out loud anyway. When he starts reading your group starts laughing. What would you do?

Write what you would do or how you would help. Explain why.

Dilemma 120: Class Bully

The end of school bell rings and you get up to leave the class. As you get out of your seat to leave, you are trying to get your books in your arms. The class bully walks up to you and pushes your books on the floor. What would you do?

Write what you would do or how you would help. Explain why.

Dilemma 121: Student Punching

In the corner of a stairwell you see a student punching another student so hard the student is crying and doubled over in pain. What would you do?

Write what you would do or how you would help. Explain why.

Dilemma 122: Stealing

It's almost time to go trick or treating and you know your mom doesn't have enough money to buy paint for your costume. You know the teacher has the right color paint in her storage cabinet so you go in the cabinet and get three jars when all the students are out of the classroom. Is this right? What would you do?

Write what you would do or how you would help. Explain why.

Dilemma 123: Lunch time

It's Friday and the lunch today is your favorite. You look ahead in the line and notice a student taking double portions and you know there is just enough food for the people who bought a ticket. What would you do?

Write what you would do or how you would help. Explain why.

Dilemma 124: Bathroom Vandalism

Mike and his friend are in the bathroom, writing on the bathroom stalls. After they go back to class, Mike starts feeling guilty and wants to apologize to the teacher. But his friend says if he tells, he would not be his friend anymore. What would you do?

Write what you would do or how you would help. Explain why.

Dilemma 125: Friend who Bullies

You have a friend who always bullies people with his words. You want to remain his friend, but you don't like how he treats people. What would you do?

Write what you would do or how you would help. Explain why.

Dilemma 126: Spit Balls

You see a student sent outside of his classroom to sit because he was throwing spit balls in class. You see him take a pen that was on the floor and start writing on the wall. What would you do?

Write what you would do or how you would help. Explain why.

Dilemma 127: Bathroom

The bathroom is loaded with kids. One student stuffs paper in the toilet, and the toilet overflows. Two students fall and hurt themselves. You know how this all started. What would you do?

Write what you would do or how you would help. Explain why.

Dilemma 128: Teacher Desk

The teacher has a basket of toys on her desk. You see Mark take a toy and put the toy in his desk. The teacher starts the next activity with the toys, but notices they are not all there. What would you do?

Write what you would do or how you would help. Explain why

Dilemma 129: Toilet Paper

You know a group of fifth-grade students are going to toilet paper the bathroom right after school. They took toilet paper out of the janitor's office and hid them in their backpacks. What would you do?

Write what you would do or how you would help. Explain why.

Dilemma 130: Gossip

You have a friend who always gossips about people. Today you heard her tell a group of students that another girl was mean and you know that girl isn't mean. What would you do?

Write what you would do or how you would help. Explain why.

Dilemma 131: Holiday Break Mishap

It's almost time for the holiday break and everyone seems excited for the break. Three boys are running down the hallway toward their class and run into a student on crutches and he falls over. The students don't stop to help but, keep running and leave the student crying for help. What would you do?

Write what you would do or how you would help. Explain why.

Dilemma 132: Snack Time Bully

It's snack time and a student wants to trade snacks with you. You say no and he starts bullying you. What would you do?

Write what you would do or how you would help. Explain why.

Dilemma 133: Bathroom Stalls

A student goes in the bathroom and sees an older student writing bad words in permanent marker on the stall doors. What would you do?

Write what you would do or how you would help. Explain why.

Dilemma 134: Spelling Test

On Friday students take the weekly spelling test. The teacher asks everyone to take out a piece of paper for the test. You glance over and see the words on the side wall. Should you tell the teacher? What would you do?

Write what you would do or how you would help. Explain why.

Dilemma 135: Screaming Boys

You enter the bathroom and find three screaming boys swinging on the bathroom doors. You try to get by them, but they try to include you in their activity. What would you do?

Write what you would do or how you would help. Explain why.

Dilemma 136: Holiday Concert

The mixed chorus is rehearsing for the holiday concert. You see a student walking away crying. You ask what's wrong, and the student says that they were laughing at her singing. What would you do?

Write what you would do or how you would help. Explain why

Dilemma 137: Running in the Hall

You see two students running in the hall and trip another student. The student falls and lands on her side breaking a rib. She screams in pain. The two students run into their classroom without helping. What could you do in this situation? What would you do?

Write what you would do or how you would help. Explain why.

Dilemma 138: Gun Bag

A student is carrying a long bag and holding it by the handle. It' looks like a gun bag and not any sports equipment. No one else is around to see it. What would you do?

Write what you would do or how you would help. Explain why.

Dilemma 139: School Bully

The school bully is making threats against a boy in a wheel chair. You know something is going to happen because you overhead the bully say it's going down today. What would you do?

Write what you would do or how you would help. Explain why.

Dilemma 140: Mean Comments

You overheard two girls make mean comments about another girl in class. These two girls always make fun of this girl, and you know it hurts the girl, because she leaves the class with tears in her eyes. What would you do?

Write what you would do or how you would help. Explain why.

Dilemma 141: Stealing

During your Halloween party you see a student stuff candy into his pocket when no one is looking. Then you see him ask the teacher for more candy. What would you do?

Write what you would do or how you would help. Explain why.

Dilemma 142: Acted Out

Luke is making a mess at his desk. The next thing you see is Luke throwing his books on the floor. He gets out of his seat and screams at the teacher, "You are awful". He then jumps back in his desk and slumps over sobbing. You know why this happened, because you saw the girl behind him mess up Luke's desk and out of frustration Luke acted out. What would you do?

Write what you would do or how you would help. Explain why.

Dilemma 143: Pokes Students

You have a student in science class who just can't sit still. She wanders the room and pokes students while the teacher is busy with other students. What would you do?

Write what you would do or how you would help. Explain why.

Dilemma 144: Front of the Lunch Line

Linda pushes her way into the front of the line during lunch. Marci has had it with her and tells her to go to the back of the line. Linda and Marci start to scream at each other and cause a scene. There is no teacher around to help with the situation. What would you do?

Write what you would do or how you would help. Explain why.

Dilemma 145: Bad Words

A girl was passes notes back and forth to a boy in class. The boy reads the last note and gets all red in the face. When he drops the note on the floor you pick it up and quickly read it. The note is filled with bad words. What would you do?

Write what you would do or how you would help. Explain why.

Dilemma 146: Cigarettes

You want to be involved with a certain group of students in your class. The students say they would accept you in the group if you smoke cigarettes in front of them at the party. Next year is middle school and you want to be included with this group of students. What would you do?

Write what you would do or how you would help. Explain why.

Dilemma 147: Lying

Tammy likes Mike and wants to sit with him at lunch. Debbie likes Mike too so she tells Mike some lies about Tammy. What would you encourage Tammy do? What would you do?

Write what you would do or how you would help. Explain why.

Dilemma 148: Team Assignment

Your class is divided into teams. One student who has a hard time grasping the directions is assigned to your team. You tell the teacher you don't want him in the team because it takes him too long to understand the directions. What would you do?

Write what you would do or how you would help. Explain why.

Dilemma 149: Teacher Desk

Your teacher goes to the front of the class to sit at her desk. You know that a student put a dead snake on her chair. What would you do?

Write what you would do or how you would help. Explain why.

Dilemma 150: Math Games

Jane loves the math games that are played in class. She decides to take one of the games home without permission from the teacher. You see this. What would you do?

Write what you would do or how you would help. Explain why.

Dilemma 151: Homework

You left your homework on your desk and ran outside for recess. When you came back your homework is gone. What would you do?

Write what you would do or how you would help. Explain why.

Dilemma 152: Learns Differently

A group of students are making fun of a student who learns differently. What would you do?

Write what you would do or how you would help. Explain why.

Dilemma 153: Recess Smoking

You are out to recess and you see two students run behind the trash bins. Within two minutes you see smoke coming from the bins and the students running away laughing. What would you do?

Write what you would do or how you would help. Explain why.

Dilemma 154: Special Pen Case

Marsha sits in the back row and has a special pencil case sitting on her desk. When students go out to recess, Marsha bumps it off her desk. As Jane walks out of the class, she picks it up and puts it in her pocket. Mike sees this all happening. What should Mike do? What would you do?

Write what you would do or how you would help. Explain why.

Dilemma 155: Substitute Teacher

Your teacher is gone for the day and you have a substitute teacher. Most of the students are throwing spit balls and laughing loudly. Do you join in? What would you do?

Write what you would do or how you would help. Explain why.

Dilemma 156: Gum Chewing

One student chew gum every day during class. When he is done chewing, he sticks the gum under his desk. What would you do?

Write what you would do or how you would help. Explain why

Dilemma 157: Struggling Friend

You best friend is struggling with a science problem and asks you to let him see your paper so he can figure out what to do. What do you do?

Write what you would do or how you would help. Explain why.

Dilemma 158: Spreading Lies

Three girls are spreading lies about another girl in your class. You know for sure what they are saying is not true. What would you do?

Write what you would do or how you would help. Explain why.

Dilemma 159: Wrong Procedure

Four students are at the white board completing a math problem. One student uses the wrong procedure to complete the problem. You can hear a student chuckling and calling him stupid. The student at the board gets so shaken by this he drops the marker and goes to his seat. After class the student is seen visibly upset. What would you do?

Write what you would do or how you would help. Explain why.

Dilemma 160: Borrows Pencils

Your friend always borrows pencils from you. Before the school day is over, he always loses them and will surely ask you again tomorrow for more pencils. Is there anyway you can help your friend with this ongoing habit? What would you do?

Write what you would do or how you would help. Explain why.

_____

_____

_____

_____

_____

_____

_____

_____

_____

_____

_____

_____

Dilemma 161: Missing Candy

You see two students eating candy that looks just like the missing candy from the teacher's desk. What would you do?

Write what you would do or how you would help. Explain why.

Dilemma 162: Reading Struggle

During a social studies lesson, a student who struggles with reading is asked to read a passage out of the text. The student stumbles on a couple of words and you hear other students laughing at him. After class the student goes out of class and can be heard saying, "I hate school, everyone picks on me." What would you do?

Write what you would do or how you would help. Explain why.

Dilemma 163: Short Skirt Test

A girl comes to school with short skirts. The teacher approaches her and tells her to kneel down on the floor. The teacher then checks the girl to see if her skirt touches the floor. The student whispers to the teacher that she has hand-me downs and that is why she has short skirts on every day. The teacher allows the student to go back to her desk. Now students are poking fun at the student for her short skirts. What would you do?

Write what you would do or how you would help. Explain why.

Dilemma 164: Gossiping

Two girls are heard gossiping about another girl. What they are saying are lies and ruining the girl's reputation. You know what they are saying isn't true, but you don't want to get involved. Then you think, "Well if they say that about her, will they say that about me someday?" What would you do?

Write what you would do or how you would help. Explain why.

Dilemma 165: Gun in School

Your school has a no-tolerance policy. You see a gun in a student's locker. What would you do?

Write what you would do or how you would help. Explain why.

Dilemma 166: School Bus

You are on the school bus and see the boy two seats ahead of you drop his gloves on the floor. The boy sitting behind him leans down and picks the gloves up and puts them in his coat pocket. The bus stops and the students get out to walk home. What would you do?

Write what you would do or how you would help. Explain why.

Dilemma 167: Rainbow Hair

A student with rainbow hair is being picked on in the hallway. What would you do?

Write what you would do or how you would help. Explain why.

Dilemma 168: Gym Class

In gym class students are poking fun at the heavy-set student. You see the student struggling with running and catching the ball. What would you do?

Write what you would do or how you would help. Explain why.

Dilemma 169: Lunch Time

At lunch you see the new student sitting alone. What would you do?

Write what you would do or how you would help. Explain why.

Dilemma 170: Stealing

Luke sees that the toys that were used as part of math class have not been put away. You watch him quietly slip four of the toys into his pocket. What would you do?

Write what you would do or how you would help. Explain why.

Dilemma 171: Learns Differently

A group of students are laughing uncontrollably in front of the classroom chalkboard. You look closely and see that a student who learns differently is struggling to complete a math problem on the board. The group of students start poking fun of the student. What would you do?

Write what you would do or how you would help. Explain why.

Dilemma 172: Lunchtime

At lunchtime you see the lunch lady go back to get more apples to hand out. You are still hungry and want to have more to eat. Do you take some potato chips while she is not looking? What would you do?

Write what you would do or how you would help. Explain why.

Dilemma 173: Pokes and Pushes

A student pokes and pushes books out of other students' hands. When confronted she says she didn't do it and that the students are just lying about her. What would you do?

Write what you would do or how you would help. Explain why.

Dilemma 174: New Library Books

The teacher finishes passing out new library books for students to look at. One student shows he doesn't like his by ripping the inside of the book. What would you do?

Write what you would do or how you would help. Explain why.

Dilemma 175: School Violence

As you are walking to school, a group of boys carrying backpacks are talking about how they would take over the school. One boy says that everything we need is in our backpack. What would you do with this information?

Write what you would do or how you would help. Explain why.

Dilemma 176: Mean Comments

A new student with a bright smile enters your classroom. Two students who are your friends start saying mean things about the student. What would you do?

Write what you would do or how you would help. Explain why.

Dilemma 177: Speech Problem

A student in your class doesn't speak clearly. Students in class make fun of him when he speaks. You know he has a speech problem and sees a teacher for this. The student is shaken up about being made fun of, but doesn't know what to do. What would you do?

Write what you would do or how you would help. Explain why.

Dilemma 178: Not Prepared

Alex is a great friend but has a bad habit of not being prepared for class. He loses all his supplies and expects you or your friends to share your supplies with him. What can you do to help John remember his supplies for class? What would you do?

Write what you would do or how you would help. Explain why.

Dilemma 179: Cheating

Lisa pulls her long sleeve shirt up to her elbows and you can see she has the list of spelling words on her underside of her forearm. As she looks at the words, you felt as if someone punched you in the stomach because you had worked so hard to learn the words, and she probably will do better on the test than you. What would you do?

Write what you would do or how you would help. Explain why.

Dilemma 180: Assignment Problem

As the teacher is handing out the completed math assignments, you are wondering what grade you would receive on the assignment because you didn't really understand it. When she approaches you and puts the assignment on your desk, you can see that it's not your assignment but someone else's. But the score on the assignment is so high you felt proud and needed a good grade. Your name was on it, but the teacher put your name on it. What would you do?

Write what you would do or how you would help. Explain why.

ABOUT THE AUTHOR

Dr. Darylann Whitemarsh is a professor at Concordia University Portland in the Doctoral Department. She has taught Character Education and Ethics at the graduate level and has trained teachers statewide in ethics and character education for the elementary, middle-school, and high school level. Dr. Whitemarsh's passion for ethics stems from thirty years of teaching middle school students and organizing and running a Character Education program. She is an award-winning teacher at the K-12 and University level, who has trained teachers across the United States in how to teach character through dilemmas to students.

A wonderful and supportive book to safely engage a young reader in challenging scenarios and guide towards a positive outcome. Taking life's challenges and learning about choices is an organic method to build character and intrinsic rewards. Dr. Whitemarsh uses her years of expertise to masterfully empower youth!

Sena Wilmoth, MS
Director, Online Academic Affairs
CU Online

In an increasingly complex world, it is good for students to have a guide who can help them develop skills for understanding and responding positively to situations that may feel overwhelming. Dr. Whitemarsh is an educator whose writing will inspire students to think critically, act respectfully, and set change in motion.

Marty A. Bullis, Ph.D.
Associate Professor of Doctoral Studies
Director of Doctoral Studies
College of Education
Concordia University Portland, Oregon.

Dr. Darylann Whitemarsh lives by strong morals and ethical standards. Her integrity, personal values, and honesty are portrayed in her daily actions, while expecting the same behaviors in the classroom. As a Concordia University Accelerated Learning faculty of the year award winner, has been a great role model for our faculty and students in her ability to demand academic excellence and provide mentorship to our students.

Tara Carr
Past Director of Concordia University Appleton Center

As a hospice volunteer counselor, Dr. Darylann Whitemarsh embodies compassion and being genuinely present in the moment. She recognizes subordinating a need for control enabling freedom to adapt to life's circumstance. These qualities shine through her tender course room conversations that influence her adult learners online to rediscover who they are first, before focusing on what they do and how they influence others. When further considering her meaningful education experience helping adolescents discover their freedom to be and to make good choices, this adds up to a lifetime of helping people of all ages and walks of life resolve personal and intimate issues set in a challenging context. I have been told to not let the moment be too big, to take it one play, one pause, one breath, one conversation at a time. Let Dr. Whitemarsh take you on a journey of powerfully being present in the pages within.

Marty Zimmerman, Med
Published Author, Leadership Coach
Core Faculty
USMC Retired

www.ingramcontent.com/pod-product-compliance
Lightning Source LLC
Chambersburg PA
CBHW081456040426
42446CB00016B/3263